The Cruise Ship

I Talk You Talk Press

Copyright © 2019 I Talk You Talk Press

ISBN: 978-4-909733-33-7

www.italkyoutalk.com

info@italkyoutalk.com

All rights reserved. No part of this publication may be resold, reproduced, stored in retrieval system, copied in any form or by any means, electronic, mechanical, photocopying, recording or otherwise transmitted without the prior written permission from the publisher. You must not circulate this publication in any format, online or otherwise.

This is a work of fiction. Names, characters, businesses, organizations, products, places, events and incidents are either the products of the author's imagination or are used in a fictitious manner. We have no affiliation with any existing companies mentioned in this story. Any resemblance to actual persons, living or dead, existing stories or actual events is purely coincidental.

Although the author and publisher have made every effort to ensure that the contents of this book were correct at press time, the author and publisher do not assume and hereby disclaim any liability to any party for any loss, damage, or disruption caused by errors or omissions, whether such errors or omissions result from negligence, accident, or any other cause.

For more information, see the Copyright Notice on our website.

Image copyright: © Netfalls #229192953 Adobe Stock Standard License

CONTENTS

Chapter One   1

Chapter Two   4

Chapter Three   6

Chapter Four   8

Chapter Five   10

Chapter Six   11

Chapter Seven   13

Chapter Eight   16

Chapter Nine   18

Chapter Ten   20

Chapter Eleven   22

Thank You   24

About the Author   26

I Talk You Talk Press

CHAPTER ONE

Sarah Lane ran out of her cabin on the luxury cruise ship. She was crying and shouting, "Where is he? Where is he?"

She ran up the stairs and went to the bar on the third floor. It was 3:00am. The bar was closed. The door was locked. She knocked on the door.

"Where is he?" she shouted loudly. A crew member was walking near the bar. He saw her.

"Madam, are you OK? What's happened?" he asked.

"You have to help me!" she said.

"OK, let's sit down and you can tell me your problem. My name is Martin. I will try to help you. What's your name?"

"Sarah Lane. My husband is Peter Lane."

He took Sarah over to an area with chairs and tables. Sarah and Martin sat down.

"It's my husband!" she said. "He's gone!"

Martin smiled. "Did he go for a walk? I'm sure he will be back soon."

"No! I haven't seen him since lunchtime yesterday! I told you! He's gone!"

Martin looked at Sarah. "I need to talk to my boss and the security guards. Come with me."

Martin helped Sarah to stand up. Her legs were very weak. She was crying loudly. They walked up some stairs and into a small office with security camera screens. "Please sit down and wait here. I will come back soon," said Martin.

Sarah sat down and cried. A few minutes later, a woman and a security guard came into the office.

"Mrs Lane. I am Claire. I am the night manager on this ship. Can you tell me your story?"

Claire and the security guard sat down on the other side of the desk. Martin closed the door and sat down next to Sarah.

Sarah began her story.

"Yesterday afternoon, we stopped in the Cayman Islands. I wanted to go sightseeing, but Peter didn't want to go. He said, 'I'm tired. I want to relax by the pool.' So I went off the ship alone. I went sightseeing and shopping for about three hours. When I came back to the boat, I went to our cabin. Peter wasn't there. I thought, *He's probably in one of the bars. He likes the bars and he likes drinking.* So I stayed in our cabin and went to sleep. I woke up and got ready for dinner. I waited for him, but he didn't come. So I had dinner alone. I thought, *This is strange. He always comes to dinner. But maybe he drank too much. Maybe he will eat some food in the bar.*

"After dinner, I walked around the ship looking for him. I went into all the bars, but he wasn't there. Then I went to the swimming pools, but he wasn't there. I couldn't find him. I thought, *Maybe he is walking around the ship, or maybe he is on one of the decks, watching the sea. He will come back later.* So I went to our cabin and waited. After a while, I fell asleep. I woke up ten minutes ago and he wasn't there."

Sarah started to cry loudly. "He still hasn't come back! It's three am! Where is he?"

Martin and Claire looked at each other. They were thinking the same thing. *Was Peter with another woman?* But, of course, they didn't say that to Sarah.

"Mrs. Lane, we will look on the security cameras. We have a very good system. We have recordings from everywhere on the ship for all day yesterday. Can you help us? Can you tell us about his clothes? What does he look like?"

"He was wearing brown shorts and a cream shirt. He is a little fat. He is fifty-five years old. This cruise is our twenty-fifth wedding anniversary vacation! We have been married for twenty-five years! We waited a long time for this cruise!"

"Mrs. Lane, I know you are worried, but can you tell us more about your husband? What colour is his hair?" asked Claire.

"He has no hair. He is bald," said Sarah.

"Which bar does he usually go to?"

"The bar on the third floor, next to the beauty salon."

The security guard started to press buttons on a computer and look at the screen.

After a few minutes, he said, "I can't see anyone who looks like your husband by the pool yesterday afternoon. Maybe he went to the bar after lunch."

Then he said, "Is this your husband?"

CHAPTER TWO

Sarah, Claire and Martin looked up at the screen. On the screen there was a man. He was wearing brown shorts and a cream shirt. He was walking into the bar. The time on the screen was 1:30pm.

"Yes! That's my husband!" said Sarah.

The security guard changed the screen to a picture inside the bar. Peter Lane sat at a table and ordered a drink. He was talking to the people next to him. One of the people was a woman. Martin and Claire looked at each other. Was Peter Lane with the woman?

At around 4:00pm, Peter walked out of the bar. The security guard changed the screen again, and they watched him walk up the stairs. They saw Peter open the door and go out onto the top deck.

Then the screen went black. Everyone looked at the security guard.

"Sorry," he said. "The camera on the top deck has been broken since yesterday. No one has been able to fix it. We have no pictures for the deck."

"The camera is broken?" shouted Sarah. "So we can't see him on the deck?"

"No, we can't see him on the deck. But we can find him leaving the deck on other cameras," said the security guard. He pressed some more keys on the computer, and a picture appeared on the screen. "This is the camera for the door. We can watch him leave the deck and go back inside."

They watched the screen for a long time. Many people went out onto the deck and went back inside, but Peter Lane didn't go back inside.

Claire, Martin and the security guard started to feel worried. Peter Lane didn't leave the deck. So, where was he?

"We check the decks every night. We didn't see anyone. I'll send someone up to the top deck to look again," said the security guard. He called another security guard.

"I'm sure everything is fine," said Claire kindly. But she was worried. Where was Peter Lane?

A few minutes later, the security guard answered his phone.

"Nothing? OK, thank you."

The security guard looked at Claire, Martin and Sarah. "Mr Lane is not on the deck," he said.

Sarah screamed. "He is in the sea! Someone killed him! Someone pushed him into the sea!" she shouted.

"Mrs Lane, I know this is very difficult for you. I'm sure no one killed your husband. But…this is a difficult question…was he happy?" asked Claire.

Sarah looked at Claire. "What do you mean? Do you think he jumped off the ship? Do you think he wanted to die? He was happy with me! Of course he was happy! He didn't want to die! He loved me! Someone killed him! Call the police! They must come now!"

"But Mrs Lane. We left the Cayman Islands at 9:00pm last night," said Claire. "We will call the police, but we are a long way away from the Cayman Islands now. Maybe they can come to the ship, or maybe the ship will have to go back to the Cayman Islands."

CHAPTER THREE

The ship's manager called the police in the Cayman Islands. The captain turned the ship around and returned to the Cayman Islands.

In the morning, the guests on the ship were very surprised when they woke up. There were police officers everywhere, and they were back in the Cayman Islands.

Police boats and rescue boats searched the water. A helicopter came. Everyone on the ship was worried. The police wanted to talk to Sarah and some other guests.

Sarah stayed in the small clinic on the ship. The doctor gave her some medicine to help her relax. But Sarah couldn't relax. "Someone killed my husband! Someone killed him!" she shouted. "Why was that security camera broken? Someone broke it, so they could kill my husband!"

The security guards and police talked to the other people who went onto the top deck. They watched the security film of the door again. Peter Lane went onto the deck alone. They looked at everyone who went onto the top deck from 1:00pm to 6:00pm. They watched everyone come back. One man walked back from the deck and into the ship at about 5:00pm. He was wearing a white T-shirt and green shorts. He was wearing a hat and glasses, and he had a camera around his neck. He had dark hair. They couldn't see this man go onto the top deck, but many people went onto the deck in large groups. Maybe he was in the middle of a large group. The police wanted to talk to this man, but there were 3,000 people on the cruise ship. It was very difficult to find him.

The Cruise Ship

They told Sarah about the man. They showed her the security film. "Do you know this man?" they asked.

"No, I don't know him. But he killed my husband!" she shouted. "He's a killer!"

"Why do you think someone killed your husband?" the police asked Sarah. "Did he have enemies?"

"No. Peter has no enemies. But he is gone. He wouldn't leave me. He would not jump into the sea. So someone killed him!"

The police watched the security cameras again. They watched the man walk around the ship. Then, he walked into an area with no security cameras.

The police checked the cabin of Mr and Mrs Lane. Peter's passport was in the cabin. His credit cards were with his passport. Where was he? Did he jump into the water? Or did someone kill him?

Everyone on the cruise ship was worried. Some people were angry. The cruise was expensive. It was their vacation. Now, they couldn't travel to the next island. The ship had to stay in the Cayman Islands while the police searched for Peter Lane.

It was a mystery. Where was he? Did he jump into the water? Who was the man in the green shorts? Did he kill Peter Lane? And where did the man in the green shorts go? The police watched many hours of security camera film, but they never saw the man in the green shorts again. Where was Peter Lane? And where was the man in the green shorts?

CHAPTER FOUR

At 9:00am, three days later, Peter Lane walked into a bank on the Cayman Islands. He looked different. He was wearing a brown wig and glasses.

"Good morning!" he said to the woman behind the counter. "My name is Stuart Stirling. I'd like to check the money in my bank account."

"I will call the manager. Please wait a moment," said the woman.

A few minutes later, the manager came out of his office.

"Good morning, Mr Stirling. Please come into my office," said the manager.

Peter Lane walked into the manager's office.

"Please sit down," said the manager. "Can I see your passport?"

"Here it is," said Peter.

"The manager looked at the passport. "May I take a copy of your passport, Mr Stirling?"

"Of course," said Peter. The manager copied the photo page of the passport, and gave it back to Peter. "Thank you, Mr Stirling." He typed on his computer and looked at the computer screen. "The money was sent from your bank account in the UK three weeks ago. Three million US dollars."

Peter Lane smiled. "Thank you," he said. "Could I take out two hundred thousand dollars?"

"Certainly." The manager went out of the office.

While Peter was waiting for his money, he thought about his plan. *I will rent a nice house on this island for a few months. I will relax and enjoy the island life. Then, after a few months, I will return to Europe. I will buy a big house in Spain. I will get a young girlfriend. Life will be great!* He thought about Sarah. *She will be OK. We had travel insurance, and I had life insurance. So she will get a lot of money from the insurance. She also has the house in England. She will be fine. I was so unhappy with her. Now, I am free!*

The manager came back to the office. "Here is your money, Mr Stirling. Please count it."

Peter counted the money. "Yes, it is fine," he said. "Thank you." He put all the money into a big bag. He walked out of the bank and into the sunny street. He could smell the sea. The wind was fresh, and the sun was hot. He smiled. *My life will be wonderful,* he thought.

CHAPTER FIVE

Peter spent the day looking at houses with a housing company. He found a nice house with views of the sea. It had five bedrooms and a swimming pool. It had a beautiful garden with many flowers. Inside, there was a refrigerator, washing machine, a sofa, chairs, tables and a TV.

"This is perfect," he said. "When can I rent it?"

"It is empty, so you can rent it from today, Mr Stirling," said the man from the housing company.

"Great," said Peter.

The next day, he checked out of his hotel and moved into the house. He went to the supermarket and bought some food and coffee. He made a cup of coffee in the kitchen and switched the TV on. The news was on. They were talking about Peter Lane. It was a mystery. The police were still looking for the man in green shorts. The cruise ship couldn't stay in the Cayman Islands, so it had gone to the next island.

Peter smiled. *I will never see Sarah again,* he thought. *The police think I am dead. They think I jumped off the ship, or someone killed me. No one will find me.*

When he finished his coffee, he went out into the garden and sat next to the swimming pool.

I'm tired today, but what shall I do tomorrow night? he thought. *I should celebrate. I will go out to a bar and drink champagne. Life is great!*

CHAPTER SIX

The next day, Peter had a relaxing time. He sat next to the pool and swam in the water. Then, he went shopping. He bought some new shirts, pants, shorts and shoes. In the evening, he put a new shirt and pants on, and he also put a blond wig on his head. In the bag he took from the cruise ship, there were three wigs – a black one, a brown one and a blond one. He went to a bar in the centre of the city.

The bar was small. There were some local people and some tourists drinking there. Peter was alone, so he sat at the bar. He ordered a glass of champagne. Many people were talking about the cruise ship. Some people said, "Someone killed Peter Lane." Other people said, "Peter Lane jumped off the ship." Peter smiled. *Only I know the truth,* he thought.

There were two tourists on his right side, and a local man on his left side. The tourists were a middle-aged man and woman from Germany.

"Excuse me," said the woman. "When you ordered your drink from the barman, I heard your accent. You are from the UK. Peter Lane was from the UK. What do you think about the story?"

"I think it is very sad," said Peter.

"It is a big story in the newspapers in the UK," said the man. "I read the newspapers on the Internet. Some people think there was a killer on the ship. It is scary."

The champagne was nice, thought Peter. *But I want a beer.* Peter ordered a beer. He didn't want to talk about the story. "So how long are you staying here?" he asked the man and woman.

"Two weeks," said the man. "It is our wedding anniversary."

"Oh, really?" said Peter. It was my wedding anniversary too, he thought. "Congratulations," he said.

"How long are you staying?" asked the woman.

"Oh, a few weeks," said Peter.

"Are you alone?"

"Yes. I don't have a wife," said Peter. He smiled again. *This feels good!* he thought. *I am single! I can do anything! Maybe I can find a girlfriend.*

They talked some more about travelling and work. The local man next to Peter started talking with them. He told them about nice places to visit on the island. Peter drank many beers. He was having a good time. The people were very friendly.

There was a TV screen above the bar. It was showing a football match. After the match, the news came on the screen. The news was about Peter Lane. The police were still searching the water. They were still looking for the man in the green shorts. There was an interview with Sarah. She was crying. She said, "My husband didn't jump off the ship. Someone killed him!" Peter was drunk. He laughed. "Maybe Peter Lane was tired after twenty-five years of marriage to you!" he said to the TV. The German couple and the local man looked at Peter strangely. The local man finished his beer.

"I have to work early tomorrow," he said. "I'm going now."

Peter and the German couple said goodbye to the man, and the man walked out of the bar.

CHAPTER SEVEN

Kevin Woods walked back to his house. *That was strange,* he thought. *The man said, 'Maybe Peter Lane was tired after twenty-five years of marriage.' How did the man know it was twenty-five years?*

Kevin was a policeman. All the police on the Cayman Islands were looking for the man in the green shorts. He went into his house, and logged on to his computer. He checked the Internet stories. The stories did not say Mr and Mrs Lane were married for 25 years. The police knew that information, but other people didn't know. So how did the man at the bar know?

Kevin switched off his computer and went to bed.

The next morning, he woke up. I have to go to work early and tell my co-workers, he thought. He had a cup of coffee, checked the newspaper, and went to work.

"Good morning. You are early," said David Parker, his boss.

"Mr Parker, I want to talk to you about Peter Lane," said Kevin. "Last night, I was in a bar. I was sitting next to a man from the UK. We were watching the story about Peter Lane on the news. The man laughed and said, 'Maybe Peter Lane was tired after twenty-five years of marriage.' How did he know it was twenty-five years?"

David looked at Kevin. "That is strange," he said. "What was the man's name?"

"I don't know. I didn't ask his name. He had blond hair and was a little fat. He was wearing a new shirt and new pants."

"New clothes?"

"Yes."

"Maybe he knows Peter Lane. Let's try to find him. Where does he live?"

"He said he is staying in a big house with a view of the ocean. He didn't say the place name. But we can contact all the housing companies. We can ask them about the people renting the houses."

"Good idea," said David. "You can do that today. Rochelle will help you."

Rochelle was a policewoman. She and Kevin waited until the housing companies were open, then they started calling them.

Kevin picked up the phone and called Nice Island Houses.

"Hello, this is Kevin Woods, from the police station."

"Ah, hello Kevin," said the man at the housing company. It was a small island, and the man knew Kevin.

"I have a question. Have you helped any men from the UK to find a house?"

"From the UK? Yes. A few days ago, a man rented a house. He moved into the house two days ago."

"What was his name?"

"Let me check…" A minute later, the man said, "Stuart Stirling."

"What did he look like?" asked Kevin.

"He had dark hair. He was a little fat. He was wearing shorts and a T-shirt."

"What colour were his shorts?" asked Kevin.

"I can't remember," said the man.

"Were they green?" asked Kevin.

"Green? I don't think so. But I don't know."

"Dark hair…hmm…did the hair look natural?"

"Natural? I think so. I don't know," said the man.

"I'd like to talk to Stuart Stirling," said Kevin. "What is his address?"

The man gave Kevin the address, and Kevin said goodbye.

"Rochelle, did you find any information?" he asked.

"No. I called all the housing companies, but no one knows about a British man."

"OK, let's find some information about Stuart Stirling," he said.

"Who is he?" she asked.

"A British man. He rented a house earlier this week."

"Does he know Peter Lane?" asked Rochelle.

"I don't know. Call immigration. I want to know when he came here. He has money. I will call all the banks. I will ask some police officers to go to the house and watch him."

Rochelle picked up her phone, and Kevin went into David's office to tell him his plan.

CHAPTER EIGHT

An hour later, Kevin and Rochelle were sitting in David's office.

"Did anyone called Stuart Stirling ask to come and stay in this country?" asked David.

"No," said Rochelle. "No one called Stuart Stirling asked for a visa to stay here. There is no record of a visitor of that name at the immigration office."

"I found the bank where Stuart Stirling has an account. I sent John to the bank for a copy of his passport. This is the copy," said Kevin. They all looked at the passport. In the passport picture, the man had dark hair.

"His hair is dark, but I'm sure it is the same man I saw in the bar last night," said Kevin.

David looked at the passport picture. Then, he looked at his computer. On his computer, there was a photograph of Peter Lane.

"Do you think he looks like Peter Lane?" he asked.

Rochelle and Kevin looked at the photograph on the computer, and then at the passport photograph.

"A little," said Rochelle.

"Do you think Stuart Stirling is Peter Lane?" asked Kevin.

"Maybe," said David.

Then, someone knocked on the door. "Come in," said David.

John walked into the office.

"Sir, I found Stuart Stirling. He was at home in his garden, having breakfast. I looked over the wall. I took a photograph. Look."

The police officers looked at John's camera. "He has no hair!"

said Kevin. "That is Peter Lane!"

"Quick! Go to the house and bring him here!" said David.

Rochelle and Kevin walked out of the office and out of the police station. They got into a police car and drove towards the house.

CHAPTER NINE

It was too hot outside, so Peter was in his living room. The air conditioner was on, and the room was cool. He was lying on the sofa. He was thinking about his future.

I will have a great life, he thought. *Maybe I can find a new wife in Spain. Do I want to get married again? Maybe not. Maybe I'll look for a girlfriend. We don't need to get married.*

Then, someone knocked on the door. Peter sat up quickly.

Who is that? he thought. He walked into the front room and looked through the window. He saw a policeman and a policewoman standing at his door.

It's the police! Why are they here? Peter was very shocked. He ran out of the room and went into the living room. He picked up his black wig and put it on his head. The police knocked on the door again.

He went to the door and opened it.

"Good morning!" he said, smiling. "How can I help you?"

Then he thought, *I know that policeman! He was in the bar last night!*

"Are you Mr Stirling?" asked Kevin.

"I am," said Peter.

"When did you enter our country?" asked Kevin.

"Er…a few weeks ago," said Peter.

"We checked. There is no record of you entering our country," said Kevin.

"Oh, that's strange," said Peter. "Maybe someone made a mistake."

"Or maybe you are Peter Lane!" said Rochelle.

Peter looked at Rochelle. He was shocked.
How did they find me? he thought.
"Peter Lane? No, of course I'm not Peter Lane," said Peter.
Kevin touched Peter's wig and pulled it off.
"Hey! You can't do that!" said Peter.
"You look like Peter Lane!" said Kevin. "You are coming with us! Get in the car!"

CHAPTER TEN

Peter was sitting at a desk in a room at the police station. David, Kevin and Rochelle were sitting opposite him.

"So, tell us the story, Peter," said David.

Peter put his head in his hands. "OK, OK," he said. "I am Peter Lane. I am married to Sarah Lane. I was unhappy. I didn't like my life with Sarah. So, I made a plan. In England, I had a company. It was an electronics company. Before I came here, I closed my company. I changed the money from pounds into US dollars. I sent the money to a bank here. It was about three million dollars. I used another name. I made a bank account in the name of Stuart Stirling. Then, I asked some bad people to make me a new passport. I said to Sarah, 'It is our twenty-fifth wedding anniversary. Let's go on a cruise.' Of course, Sarah said, 'yes'. She was very happy. So we went on a cruise. When the cruise ship came to the Cayman Islands, I broke one of the security cameras on the top deck of the ship. I know about technology and electronics, so it was easy for me. I put new clothes and wigs in my bag. When the ship stopped here, Sarah got off the ship to go sightseeing. I went to the bar. Then, I went to the deck. I knew the security camera was broken. I waited until I was alone, then I changed my clothes. I threw my old clothes into the sea. Then, I put on a black wig, and went back into the ship. I went to the toilets in another part of the ship. I changed my shorts again and put on a blond wig. Then, I left the ship.

"I used my new passport, my Stuart Stirling passport, and found a hotel. I stayed there for a few nights. The cruise ship came back, but then it left the Cayman Islands. I went to the bank. I got some of my money and rented a big house."

"But what was your final plan?" asked Rochelle. "You couldn't stay here. This is a small island."

"My final plan was to go to Spain. I wanted to buy a big house in Spain, get a new girlfriend and enjoy my life." Peter looked at the police officers. "I was so unhappy with Sarah. You don't understand."

"So why didn't you get divorced?" asked Rochelle. "Why did you do this?"

"Because I didn't want to give Sarah half of my money!" said Peter. "I worked hard in England for my money. Sarah didn't do anything. She went shopping every week. She bought many expensive things. She didn't work. But she always said to me, 'work more! Get me more money!' Life with Sarah was hard. I wanted to escape. So, I made this plan."

"Well it was a bad idea," said David.

"I know. I'm sorry. What will happen to me?" asked Peter.

"You made a lot of trouble for us. We spent a lot of time searching for you. You used a different passport. You used a different name to open a bank account. You did bad things Mr Lane. I think you will stay on this island for a long time. But not in your house. In jail!"

CHAPTER ELEVEN

Peter sat in the cell in jail. There were five other men in the cell. It was his second week in the jail.

"Excuse me," said Peter to a guard. "I want to speak to my wife. She is in England now. Can I call her?"

"You can call her later," said the guard. "Telephone time is from three pm."

Peter waited until 3:00pm. He didn't talk to the other men in the cell. He just sat on his bed and thought about his life.

Maybe Sarah can help me, he thought. *I will say 'sorry', and ask her for help. She loves me. She will help me.*

At 3:00pm, the guard said to Peter, "You can call your wife now." He unlocked the cell door and Peter walked out of the cell. He went to the phone and called Sarah.

"Sarah? It's me," he said.

"What do you want?" asked Sarah. She sounded angry.

"I want to say I'm sorry. I made a mistake. Can you help me?"

Sarah laughed. "Help you? You did a very bad thing. Of course I can't help you!"

"But, do you still love me?" asked Peter.

"Love you? I hate you!" shouted Sarah. "I have spoken to a lawyer. I want a divorce!"

"Divorce? No Sarah, please! I love you!" Peter said. He didn't want to get divorced. He wanted Sarah to help him.

"Well, it is too late," said Sarah. "I need to get divorced because I have a new man!"

The Cruise Ship

"What?" Peter could not believe it.

"Yes. On the ship, a nice young man called Martin helped me. He was very kind to me. We fell in love. I'm going to marry Martin, and we are going to live in Spain! Goodbye!"

Sarah put the phone down. Peter looked at the phone for a long time. Then the guard said, "Time up! Go back to your cell!"

Peter walked back to his cell slowly. He walked into the cell and looked around. *This is my future,* he thought. *I have lost everything.*

THANK YOU

Thank you for reading The Cruise Ship. (Word count: 5,056) We hope you enjoyed it.

There are quizzes about this book on our free study site I Talk You Talk Press EXTRA. http://italk-youtalk.com

If you would like to read more graded readers, please visit our website http://www.italkyoutalk.com

Other Level 2 graded readers include
Adventure in Rome
Andre's Dream
A Passion for Music
Christmas Tales
Danger in Seattle
Don't Come Back
Finders Keepers…
Hunted in Hong Kong
Marcy's Bakery
Men's Konkatsu Tales
Salaryman Secrets!
Stories for Halloween
The Perfect Wedding
The House in the Forest
The School on Bolt Street

The Cruise Ship
Train Travel
Trouble in Paris
Women's Konkatsu Tales

ABOUT THE AUTHOR

I Talk You Talk Press is a Japan-based publisher of language textbooks, graded readers and language learning/teaching resources.

Our team is made up of highly experienced language teachers and translators, who have all studied at least one additional language to an advanced level.

This experience enables us to design our materials from the perspective of both the teacher and the learner. We consult with both teachers and language learners when designing our textbooks and graded readers, and test our materials extensively in the classroom before publication.

We are a fast-growing press, and currently publish graded readers for learners of English. We publish new graded readers monthly.

www.ingramcontent.com/pod-product-compliance
Lightning Source LLC
Chambersburg PA
CBHW031440040426
42444CB00006B/904